Original title:
Life's Questions, Answered by Pancakes

Copyright © 2025 Creative Arts Management OÜ
All rights reserved.

Author: Lila Davenport
ISBN HARDBACK: 978-1-80566-016-3
ISBN PAPERBACK: 978-1-80566-311-9

A Recipe for Riddles

What comes round and fluffy,
Solves woes in a stack?
Maple or syrupy,
Sentiments never lack.

When breakfast feels heavy,
And questions start to swell,
Just flip it, get ready,
With batter, all is well.

Comfort in Every Bite

Feeling lost in the morning,
With worries on your plate?
A pancake's soft adorning,
   Turns sorrow into fate.

With butter melting slowly,
And smiles shared in the air,
Each bite feels more jolly,
Like laughter, light, and rare.

The Art of Topping Thoughts

Should I go left or right?
A dollop clears my mind.
With berries, what a sight!
I savor every kind.

Whipped cream dreams delight me,
Decisions fade away,
Each topping is a key,
To cheer up my long day.

Savoring Simple Answers

Questions rise like bubbles,
In batter, they take flight.
With flavors, squash your troubles,
And watch your worries kite.

So if the world's a mess,
Just whisk a quick retreat,
A golden, warm caress,
Wrapped in warmth, oh so sweet.

Fluffy Insights

What's the secret to all joy?
Just flip those cakes, oh boy!
Butter sizzles, syrup pours,
In every bite, the answer soars.

Does love come with a side of jam?
Or maybe with a dollop of ham?
Each taste reveals a truth untold,
In golden rounds, the wisdom's gold.

Maple Musings

Why's the sky so big and wide?
Pancakes hold the dreams inside.
With every stack, a cloud to share,
Maple whispers fill the air.

What's the best way to find cheer?
Just ask the batter, it will hear.
With syrup drizzled, life is sweet,
Every pancake makes us complete.

Circle of Understanding

Is happiness just round and flat?
Like a pancake on a mat?
Flip it over, see its face,
Understanding finds its place.

What warms the heart on a cold day?
A stack of joy, hip-hip hooray!
With every bite, we break the crust,
In circles, our thoughts are a must.

The Golden Ratio of Enlightenment

What's the secret to perfect bliss?
It's found in butter's creamy kiss.
With pancakes stacked in perfect rows,
Life's mysteries, the batter knows.

Are there answers beneath the heat?
Just taste the joy, it's oh-so-sweet!
In every layer lies the truth,
Pancakes offer wisdom's proof.

The Essence of Enjoyment

Fluffy stacks on a plate,
Maple syrup, oh what fate!
Whisk the troubles out the door,
With each bite, we laugh and soar.

Golden brown and oh so neat,
Each pancake brings a tasty treat.
Flip the worry, serve it right,
Joy is found in every bite.

Round Plates, Round Questions

Why do we ask, what is the key?
When pancakes flip, we feel so free.
Round and soft, they hold our dreams,
In syrup rivers, laughter streams.

Questions swirl like butter's glide,
Presented warm, we cannot hide.
On a plate, they gently spin,
Round and round, let joy begin.

Toppings on Tomorrow

Whipped cream clouds and berry skies,
Every forkful elicits sighs.
Fruit and chocolate, sprinkle cheer,
A feast for now, the future near.

What will we top our dreams today?
Each choice is sweet, let's not delay.
Tomorrow's hopes with syrup blend,
On tasty notes, we can depend.

The Palate of Possibilities

Pancakes stacked to greet the day,
Open hearts find what they weigh.
Options flutter, flavors play,
On a platter, fun's underway.

With each bite, we write our tune,
Sweet or savory, morning's boon.
In the rhythm of our feast,
Possibilities never ceased.

Breakfast Musings

Is syrup the answer or just a bright tease?
Flipping flapjacks, it's hard to appease.
Maple or chocolate, what tickles my fancy?
Choices like pancakes, how utterly chancy.

Do eggs have feelings when whisked in a bowl?
Or is breakfast slang for a morning role?
Hashbrowns in chaos, a crispy delight,
In the mornings of laughter, we take flight.

A Stack of Possibilities

A tower of pancakes, a sweet mountain high,
Each layer holds wonders, oh me, oh my!
Blueberries whisper secrets, cinnamon sings,
In this breakfast quest, a new day springs.

A drizzle of honey, a sprinkle of bliss,
Each bite is a puzzle, a morning to kiss.
With butter that melts like dreams on a plate,
I ponder the world, while I slowly sate.

Griddle Hues

Golden brown, crispy, what colors to choose?
Each pancake a canvas, no chance to lose.
Flipping the script on what's hot and what's not,
Why ponder my future when I've got this pot?

An array of toppings, bright berries and cream,
Every bite's a moment, a thick, tasty dream.
Should I chase the pancakes, or let them chase me?
Oh, the griddle of wisdom, it's hard to foresee.

Tickling Taste Buds with Truth

Do pancakes hold answers or just fill the void?
A breakfast rebellion, slightly overjoyed.
Mapping my mornings with fluffiness wide,
Each forkful of truth, I cheerfully ride.

With laughter and syrup, we toast to the dawn,
In the land of hot cakes, we shall carry on.
So here's to the batches that bring us delight,
In this fluffy adventure, we'll take flight!

Round and Delicious Insights

Flapjacks flip, what's at stake?
Batter dreams on a hot griddle bake.
Syrup rivers flow down the stack,
Warmth and laughter, never look back.

Golden circles tell tales anew,
Toppings sprinkle joy, oh so true.
Who needs answers, just take a bite,
Breakfast giggles, morning's delight.

Pouring Wisdom

Pour it slow, let the magic spread,
A sizzle echo fills up your head.
Confusion melts with butter's grace,
Each pancake flip, a saving embrace.

Syrup drips, coating thoughts so sweet,
With every layer, life's questions retreat.
Whisk together dreams and a hint of cheer,
A stack of wisdom, bright and clear.

Tantalizing Truths

Fluffy rounds on a breakfast plate,
Grinning at you like a happy fate.
Maple secrets in each soft bite,
Waffles wish they could have this height.

Toppings tell tales of joy and strife,
Whipped cream clouds lighten our life.
With every forkful, chuckles arise,
Fried philosophy in syrupy skies.

A Griddleful of Ideas

On the griddle, the world is spun,
Ideas bubble, oh what fun.
Flavors clash in a savory dance,
Each pancake serves a daring chance.

Plates piled high with warmth and care,
Life's tricky quandaries laid bare.
Butter melting with each silly thought,
A feast of fun, joyfully sought.

Culinary Clarity

When the pancake turns golden, truth starts to rise,
Syrup drips down, sweetening the lies.
Flip it with flair, see the edges turn bright,
In a stack of confusion, breakfast brings light.

Stacked high on my plate, thoughts start to clear,
With each fluffy layer, I laugh at my fear.
Bites of wisdom melt, with butter on top,
Encouragement served, who could ever swap?

Batter Drops of Knowledge

Whisking away doubts, I mix in the fun,
Flour and sugar dance, it's a delicious run.
Questions like bubbles, they rise and they pop,
In the batter of breakfast, we can't let them stop.

A splash of vanilla, a dash of delight,
An answer takes shape, as morning turns bright.
Pour it with laughter, each scoop tells a tale,
With pancakes a-flipping, you'll never derail!

The Art of Flipping

With a flick of the wrist, life's troubles can sway,
Pancakes are the canvas where questions can play.
The first one may flop, but don't lose your cheer,
For pancake perfection, practice is key here.

Twirling and swirling, I catch them on high,
With syrupy wisdom, I'll never say goodbye.
So let's round up friends, with a griddle and grin,
In the art of great flipping, we're destined to win!

Round Table of Truths

Gather around, folks, for a pancake pow-wow,
The syrupy truth is, we live in the now.
With each golden disc, wisdom flows free,
Conversations get fluffy, just like my tea.

At this round table, opinions stack high,
Toppings for all, so let's give it a try.
Whipped cream debates and berry-blushed smiles,
In the world of pancakes, we'll travel for miles.

Warm Embraces of Understanding

In the morning sun, I stand,
With a skillet in my hand.
Flipping dreams, a perfect stack,
Butter melts; we won't look back.

Syrup rivers, laughter flows,
Each golden layer, wisdom grows.
Questions linger, doubts collide,
One bite in, and fears subside.

Drizzled smiles on fluffy cakes,
Cooked up wisdom, no mistakes.
Bite by bite, my questions fade,
In pancake worlds, I'm not afraid.

So when in doubt, just take a seat,
Grab a fork; it's time to eat.
The answers swirl in every bite,
Pancake love makes everything right.

Sifted Thoughts

In a bowl, I sift my mind,
Flour flying, truth to find.
Whisking worries, batter thick,
For every doubt, a pancake trick.

Eggs are scrambled, thoughts go round,
In this breakfast, peace is found.
Mixing fun with heavy cares,
Every flip, a fresh perspective shares.

Pouring dreams onto the heat,
Watch them rise, my troubles beat.
Maple syrup drips like grace,
In pancake realms, I find my place.

So if you're lost, just take a peek,
In pancake wisdom, answers speak.
With every bite, you'll surely see,
Delicious truths are meant to be.

Butterin the Brain

With a pat of butter, thoughts refine,
Slathered dreams on pancakes shine.
As I munch, my worries wane,
Joy and giggles fill the grain.

Melted magic on the plate,
Transforming all I contemplate.
Questions swirl like butter's fate,
In each pancake, I relate.

Toppings stacked to greet the day,
Whipped cream clouds to float away.
Finding answers in the fluff,
Life is sweet when things get tough.

So dollop joy on every slice,
In pancake moments, life's quite nice.
With laughter shared, the world is bright,
In buttery bites, all feels right.

Pancake Paths

On a griddle, paths unfold,
Stories waiting to be told.
Each pancake, a journey shared,
With syrup trails, we're prepared.

Round and round, the batter rolls,
A roundabout of tasty goals.
Questions answered one by one,
With every flip, we have our fun.

In golden circles, life we trace,
Pancake wisdom sets the pace.
Gather 'round for breakfast time,
With laughter bubbling, all's sublime.

So tread lightly on this quest,
A plate of joy, you'll feel the best.
For on this path of tasty art,
Pancakes warm the hungry heart.

The Griddle of Inquiry

Flapjacks flip when thoughts run wild,
Syrup drips like answers compiled.
Butter melts all fears away,
Crunchy edges, come what may.

Stack them high, make it a tower,
Each bite brings a brand new power.
What's the meaning? Just taste and see,
With every bite, you're just so free.

Batter's Reflection

In mixing bowls, my worries blend,
Eggs and milk, a perfect friend.
Do I flip or do I fold?
Pancakes whisper secrets told.

Sizzle here, a bubble there,
Flapjack wisdom fills the air.
What's the recipe for a good laugh?
It's a dash of joy, a pinch of craft.

Maple Syrup Secrets

Drizzled truths in syrupy lines,
Sticky dilemmas, oh how they shine!
Pour on kindness, let it flow,
Sweeten up the woes we know.

What's the secret to a sunny day?
A golden drizzle, come what may.
Each drop a giggle, laughter obeys,
In the breakfast feast, worries glaze.

Whisking Through Wonders

With a whisk, I spin my thoughts,
Pancakes rise, and questions caught.
Fluffy dreams, in batter they hide,
Stirring up the joy inside.

What's the answer to a frown?
A pancake party, let's bring it down!
Flip them high and watch them soar,
In pancake wonder, who could want more?

Hot Cakes and Heavy Hearts

When mornings feel like heavy skies,
A stack of joy begins to rise.
Flip them over, make them golden,
With syrup dreams, the heart's beholden.

Problems seem to melt away,
Like butter on a sunny day.
With each bite, a giggle sprouts,
And worries? Just some gooey routes.

A sprinkle here, a dash of fun,
With every fork, new battles won.
What weighs you down? Just take a bite,
And let your soul find fluffy light.

Round Reflections

In life, we flip and try to land,
Like pancakes sliding on the pan.
Each round a chance, each trial a taste,
With every flop, there's no time to waste.

Reflect on days that stack so high,
Sweet memories, and syrupy sighs.
For every flip, a lesson learned,
Through crisp edges, our passion burned.

The laughter bubbles, the butter sizzles,
In morning's warmth, the joy just drizzles.
What's the secret? Just be brave,
And with each bite, your heart will save.

The Essence of Batter

What's the secret? It's in the mix,
A dash of hope, a sprinkle of tricks.
Blending woes with milk and flour,
    Creating joy in every hour.

When troubles rise like batter froths,
Just grab a whisk and stir those thoughts.
    In every lump, a little thrill,
Bake your dreams with butter still.

Pour it out, see what you've made,
A masterpiece on a plate displayed.
With syrup rivers, life's so grand,
    In every bite, take a stand.

Sweet Surrender on a Dish

So stack them high, a sweet delight,
With every layer, take a bite.
Surrender fears like butter melts,
In pancake dreams, the joy is felt.

A drizzle here, a topping there,
With laughter, spice, and not a care.
The plate's a canvas, vibrant, bold,
Each syrup swirl, like stories told.

So when the world feels heavy, gray,
Trade your worries for this buffet.
In sweet surrender, we delight,
With pancakes served, everything's bright.

The Comforting Flip

When syrup drips and butter pools,
I ponder deep like all the fools.
Is this breakfast or some kind of art?
With every bite, I feel the heart.

In stacks they rise, a fluffy dream,
Each layer holds a secret theme.
What answers lie in flour and eggs?
Perhaps I'll find them when it begs.

A sizzle sings, a golden hue,
Do pancakes know what's best to do?
They smile soft as morning light,
Whispering truths that feel just right.

So when I'm lost, confused, or glum,
I turn to griddle, wait for yum.
For in each bite, a riddle's spun,
Turns out, it's all just a morning fun!

Pancake Perspectives

In golden rounds, a world unfolds,
Each bite's a tale that's yet untold.
Do they understand my daily strife?
Or just flip themselves—oh, what a life!

With every pancake comes a thought,
Are these the answers that I sought?
They're fluffy philosophers on my plate,
Syrup sages discussing fate.

What's the meaning of this sweet stack?
A breakfast guide that won't turn back.
Do they dream of syrup rivers wide?
In fluffy landscapes—what's there to hide?

So when I chew and start to muse,
Are they wise or just sweet to choose?
Maybe the truth is sweet and round,
In batter's depths, answers abound!

Breakfast Beneath the Surface

Underneath that crispy crust,
Lies a world that's filled with trust.
Do pancakes hold the secrets vast?
Or do they just become breakfast fast?

A buttery melt, they sing to me,
What deeper lessons can there be?
Beneath the syrup's sticky guise,
Are answers hiding, oh so sly?

With every bite, I dig for gold,
What stories in these layers bold?
A fluffy riddle, let's unmask,
Can batter help with what I ask?

Yet still, they wait, a humble crew,
Just savored by the likes of you.
In breakfast joy, we find our way,
And leave the mysteries for another day!

Fluffy Doubts

As I toss that batter high,
I wonder where my dreams may fly.
Do pancakes ever doubt their fate?
Or just accept it's never late?

In every stack, a fluffy fear,
What if I'm just lost right here?
Are they the key to happiness?
Or just a cover for my stress?

With chocolate chips or fruit to share,
Am I too serious? Do I dare?
To flip my thoughts like pancakes round,
And ponder what's back on the ground?

So when I chew and smile wide,
Do these sweet treats help to decide?
Perhaps the answers lie in fun,
And worry melts like butter—done!

Pancake Prose

Flipping flapjacks at dawn's break,
Searching for answers with every shake.
Syrup flows sweet, like truth we seek,
In batter we trust, the tasty mystique.

Stack them high, like dreams on a plate,
Each bite reveals what we contemplate.
Some are fluffy, some might fall,
But isn't it fun to devour them all?

Sizzling Insights

On the griddle where they dance and sway,
Questions bubble, then fade away.
A sprinkle of salt, a dash of glee,
Making sense of our recipe.

Bubbles form like thoughts in the air,
Worries dissolve, they vanish with flair.
Each round creation, a roundabout way,
To savor the answers and flip them all day.

The Wisdom in Whipping

Whisking it good, don't you agree?
The key to life is light and free.
Add some sugar, a splash of levity,
Mix in laughter, that's the recipe!

When problems rise like dough on the verge,
Just pour some batter, let creativity surge.
Cook until golden, then serve it warm,
In each crispy corner, a thought may transform.

Sweet Resolutions

With every bite, discover the why,
Pancakes serve more than a simple fry.
They crumble fears and stack up delight,
Bringing joy in a syrupy bite.

So next time you ponder, just take a break,
Savor the moment, enjoy what you make.
Flip those worries into something neat,
And savor the sweetness that can't be beat!

Flapjacks and Philosophy

In the skillet they sizzle, round and sweet,
Thoughts of pancakes dance, a breakfast treat.
Why do we ponder, when we can just eat?
With syrup rivers flowing, oh, what a feat!

Flip the disc of wisdom, golden and bright,
What's the purpose? Butter, take flight!
Questions dissolve in each fluffy bite,
Who knew philosophy could taste so right?

The Syrup of Serenity

Pour the syrup slowly, like time on a clock,
Sticky situations? Just give them a shock.
Life's ups and downs, a pancake's block,
With each sweet drizzle, we gently unlock.

Are we all just toppings on a buttered base?
A dash of spice, a bit of grace.
Riddle me this over pancake embrace,
Finding peace in syrup, in this silly race.

When Batter Meets Bravery

Brave little batter in the bowl so bold,
Facing the heat, it's a story untold.
With a whisk of courage, it's time to unfold,
Into a pancake, a sight to behold.

What if the flip goes wrong, oh dear?
Laughter erupts, no need for fear.
In the kitchen of chaos, we all cheer,
Don't take life too serious; just add some beer!

Whisking Through Wonder

Whisking and swirling, oh what a scene,
Creating fluffiness, like we've never seen.
Are our dreams batter or just in between?
In a world of toppings, we can be keen!

Incredible flavors filled with delight,
Blueberries or chocolate, which is more right?
Life's conundrums, solved with a bite,
Laughter spills over, morning's pure light!

Pancakes of Perspective

What's the meaning of it all, we ponder,
In a stack of syrupy grace down yonder.
Flipping thoughts like a pancake so round,
Each layer reveals what we've missed, profound.

Smothered in butter, sweet dreams arise,
A sprinkle of laughter, truth in disguise.
With every bite, a new lesson unfolds,
Life's mysteries wrapped in warm, golden folds.

Golden Circles of Wisdom

Round and round we chase what we seek,
In each fluffy circle, the answers peek.
Map out your toppings, don't leave them to chance,
Sprinkle on joy, give your heart a dance.

Each bite a riddle, each syrupy stream,
Hints of enlightenment drip from the dream.
Stack it up neatly, let questions unwind,
In golden delights, all the truths you will find.

Soft and Fluffy Revelations

Soft like a cloud, wisdom rests on the plate,
A flip of the wrist can decide your fate.
With berries and cream, make it not so bland,
Life's fluffy lessons, sweetly planned.

Each forkful of comfort, a clue to behold,
Dousing with syrup, let the stories unfold.
Pancakes might giggle, as they share their plight,
Laughing at troubles, from morning till night.

The Breakfast Beacon

In the dawn's soft light, a beacon so bright,
Sizzling on griddle, what a wonderful sight.
When life gives you lemons, just turn up the heat,
Make pancakes instead, they can't be beat!

Maple-sweet wisdom drizzles like fate,
Laughter and giggles dance on your plate.
In the circle of breakfast, we chuckle and sigh,
With pancakes for wisdom, we'll reach for the sky.

The Palette of Life

In the morning, colors swirl,
On the griddle, dreams unfurl.
Batter thick as hopes once were,
Flavored thoughts in joyful blur.

Syrup flows like laughter sweet,
Every flip, a new heartbeat.
Choco chips like midnight stars,
Pancake plates heal all our scars.

Maple whispers 'Have no fear',
With each bite, the path is clear.
Butter melts, the tension's gone,
A breakfast tune, a silly song.

So taste the joy, embrace the fun,
With every pancake, life's a pun!
In syrupy pools, we find our way,
Each golden round a bright new day.

Flipping Perspectives

Life's a griddle, hot and round,
With every flip, new truths are found.
Spatula poised, what's next to rise?
Pancake wisdom, the ultimate prize.

Twirling batter, like fate it swirls,
Each layer flips, a world unfurls.
Stack 'em high, don't let dreams flop,
In syrupy pools, we learn to stop.

Blueberries burst with joy on top,
While whipped cream dances, never stops.
With every bite, laugh lines deepen,
What was serious, now a beacon.

So gather round, with friends to share,
A fluffy feast, no empty stare.
For every problem, there's a plan,
Just flip it over, and take a stand.

Flapjack Philosophy

Rise and shine, let's hit the griddle,
Pancakes serve wisdom, oh so brittle.
Golden circles on a plate in hand,
Each one a thought, sweet and planned.

Share your stack, don't eat alone,
With syrupy hugs, all worries flown.
Is it flat or fluffy? Who can say?
Let's live it up, come what may!

Chocolate drizzle, a splash of fun,
Every pancake, a laugh begun.
Flip the doubts, and take a chance,
In butter pools, we learn to dance.

So grab a fork, no need to brood,
Pancakes turn frowns to happy mood.
In this kitchen, no question's odd,
Just serve it up, a feast of God.

Syrupy Solutions

Got a problem? Grab a pan,
Pour that batter, be the fan.
Watch it bubble, let it rest,
With every flip, you'll feel the zest.

Maple syrup's thick embrace,
In sticky moments, find your grace.
Whisk your worries into the mix,
With each round, life's little tricks.

Laughter echoes, friends unite,
Over pancakes, hearts feel light.
Afraid of heights? Just stack them high,
With a dash of courage, touch the sky.

So here's the secret, a simple rule,
When life gets tough, just play it cool.
In every batter, a lesson's gleam,
Pour it out, and chase your dream.

Golden Griddle Gains

Why are mornings filled with cheer?
The golden griddle is right here!
Flipping dreams with joy and flair,
Each round delight, the weight we bear.

Mysteries of syrup's flow,
What makes the heart feel all aglow?
A drizzle here, a dab right there,
Life's dilemmas lost in air!

Do shadows linger, are they sweet?
Or is it just your breakfast treat?
Raise a fork to greet the dawn,
A crispy smile, the worries gone.

When is the right time to just flip?
When life feels like a roller trip?
Just add some butter, take a bite,
Laugh it off, it feels so right!

Top of the Stack

In the morning, who feels blue?
It's pancake time, the skies are blue!
Stack them high, let laughter rise,
With every bite, the spirit flies.

Questions come like falling crumbs,
Yet all they bring are happy drums.
What's the secret? What's the score?
A pancake feast, who could want more?

If sorrow sneaks in, just say no,
A pancake tower steals the show.
With whipped cream mountains, dreams in sight,
Life's just better when it's light!

So come and gather, share the plate,
A crispy edge can help create.
The answers mix with maple sighs,
In fluffy bites, true wisdom lies!

A Syrupy Synopsis

What's the plot? Who needs a script?
Pour some syrup, make it flipped!
The best stories start with smiles,
Fluffy fun, let's stretch for miles.

Are we lost in a world of dough?
With butter melting, worries go.
A sprinkle here, a fruit parade,
Every layer sunlight made.

Is it fate or just good taste?
Pancakes answer, never waste.
With laughter bubbling, let's explore,
Every bite's a tale, and more!

Acid thoughts? Just toss them high!
A pancake flips, and so do I.
Life's better served on every plate,
In syrupy smiles, we celebrate!

Toppings of Thought

What do you want, dear brain of mine?
A dash of nuts? Or fruit that's fine?
With sprinkles bringing joy in stacks,
The toppings sway away our hacks.

Is it gumption or is it zest?
With every bite, it's laughter's nest.
Berries burst with tales of glee,
In fluffy rounds, we find the key.

Why is syrup like a hug?
Sticky notes on this life bug.
With every swirl, our troubles dissolve,
In pancake wisdom, we evolve.

So grab a plate and join the cheer,
With every stack, there's love right here.
Toppings bright, they reappear,
In pancake realms, let's persevere!

The Perfect Stack

In the morning light they rise,
Fluffy clouds that touch the skies.
Maple syrup rivers flow,
Why's the toast always feeling low?

Each flapjack's a cause for cheer,
With every bite, worries disappear.
Can pancakes solve your troubles today?
Just take a fork and dig away!

A sprinkle of joy in each delight,
Can you live without this fluffy bite?
Stack them high, with butter and zest,
Isn't breakfast the ultimate test?

From golden browns to crispy ends,
They hold the secrets, my dear friends.
Who knew the world could be so sweet?
When pancakes make life feel complete!

Bittersweet Bites

Chocolate chips and stories told,
Each pancake a memory to behold.
What's your secret for a happy heart?
Maybe it's syrup that plays a part?

Tangled flavors in every stack,
Burnt edges bless me, no taste I lack.
Do we fuel dreams with each batter swirl?
Or find wisdom in that joyful whirl?

Biting into the sweet and the strange,
Do we wonder if pancakes can change?
A pinch of salt for life's finest mix,
Flipping fortunes with pancake tricks!

Savoring joys that sometimes clash,
Finding smiles in maple splash.
Is laughter the syrup that sweetens the deal?
With every fork, we find what's real!

Flavors of Questioning

Cinnamon whispers in the pan,
Creating currents, no master plan.
What flavor suits you, kind sir?
Do fruits make you dance, or just purr?

From lemon zest to blueberry skies,
Pancakes wear masks and clever lies.
Do they hold truths in their syrupy depths?
Or are they just breakfast's clever sheaths?

Like the morning sun, they awaken cheer,
With puddles of butter, spreading near.
Should we ponder or simply feast?
In every bite, joy is released!

Mix in some laughter, a dash of grace,
With each pancake, we embrace.
Could every question find its answer soon,
In the joy of a breakfast tune?

Seeking Whimsy in Wheat

Flour rains down like a gentle hug,
In this frolicking dough, we feel the tug.
Can a pancake make your heart take flight?
Or provoke thoughtful musings late at night?

Whisking dreams with every turn,
In the skillet, watch the magic burn.
Do plates of joy canvas our fate?
Or is it just hunger we celebrate?

Oh, golden stacks; so soft, so round,
For joy and laughter, they astound.
Can life be as simple as butter and glaze?
When pancakes dance in a syrupy haze?

Seek the whimsy; let flavors play,
Breathe in the morning and savor the day.
Will we ever find answers so sweet?
With pancakes beneath, life is a treat!

Syrup-Drenched Dilemmas

When breakfast calls with a sizzle,
You ponder love, work, and a drizzle.
But stack them up, let the sweet flow,
Pancakes provide answers you know.

What's the meaning of this grind?
A flapjack flip can ease the mind.
With butter melting, all is bright,
Each bite reveals a truth in sight.

When syrup pools, do not despair,
Dig deep for thoughts that others share.
A fluffy bite dispels the gloom,
In pancake world, there's always room.

So grab your fork, let's make it quick,
With every slice, find the magic trick.
For in the round and golden treat,
Lies every answer, warm and sweet.

The Flip Side of Existence

In a frying pan, the world spins round,
Life's secret answers can easily be found.
Flip it over, see what's beneath,
Pancakes share wisdom, sweet and sheathe.

A sprinkle here, a dash of that,
Questions rise high, like flour in chat.
What's the purpose, you might ask?
It's all in the pancake-making task.

Stack them up, see what they tease,
With chocolate chips, or nuts, if you please.
What's the fate of love, you ponder?
Just pour on syrup, and let thoughts wander.

In every bite, flavors collide,
The truths of life, they do not hide.
So take a bite, and you just might see,
The flip side of existence, so carefree.

Cooking Up Clarity

Mixing batter in a big bowl,
Stirring up questions of the soul.
What's the deal with dreams and schemes?
Pancakes serve clarity on a plate of cream.

A pinch of salt, a dash of cheer,
While cooking, the answers become clear.
Is it joy you seek, or just a thrill?
Pour some syrup, and find your will.

Flipping cakes on a griddle hot,
Each turn reveals what was forgot.
What's success, if not a stack?
With butter melting, you'll have no lack.

So when you're lost, don't hesitate,
Grab a plate, it's never too late.
For in the art of making bites,
You'll find insights that feel just right.

Forkfuls of Reflection

With every forkful come thoughts anew,
Life's queries swirl like morning dew.
Why do we worry? What's the fuss?
Just stack those cakes, and ride the bus.

Pancakes warm, fresh from the heat,
With each sweet layer, life feels complete.
What's the trick to happiness, friend?
A drizzle of syrup can surely lend.

Take a bite, let flavors burst,
In moments of doubt, pancake's a must.
Is it peace you seek? Or perhaps a sign?
Find meaning in maple, taste the divine.

So serve them up, and let's all feast,
On forkfuls of joy, to say the least.
For reflection served on a buttery round,
Will lift you up, where wisdom's found.

The Pancake Paradox

Why do we flip? Is it for fun?
Or to see gravity lose to the run?
Fluffy stacks rise, hopes collide,
In syrupy pools, our dreams must glide.

Do we stack high or keep it low?
A tower of joy, a waffle will show!
A crispy edge, a soft little heart,
With butter and laughter, let's start!

Golden brown smiles, are they really real?
Or just batter dreams on a breakfast wheel?
With toppings that fly, we should take a chance,
As we flip through the day, let's eat and dance.

Pour out the syrup, let worries dissolve,
Mysteries crepe up, but we'll solve!
So in a short stack or a grand buffet,
We find the answers in every way.

Drizzled Doubts

Is it a pancake or a sad flat cake?
With a drizzle of doubt, the world starts to shake!
What do the eggs think, all whisked in a bowl?
Do they dream of the frying, or just want their role?

A dollop of cream, like a question in jest,
Do bubbles from batter mean we're blessed?
As we smother the stack with sweet maple cheer,
It seems all our worries just disappear!

Who put the peanut butter in our plight?
A nutty conundrum that feels just not right?
Yet with toast on the side, we'll figure it out,
Pancakes are heroes in our morning shout!

Stack them around, let's ponder the griddle,
In laughter and syrup, life's woes turn little!
For every flip, a new giggle so grand,
With spatulas ready, take a stand!

Comfort from the Kitchen

The kitchen's a stage, where pancakes are stars,
They dance on the griddle, just like guitars.
In warm, buttery hugs, we seek our relief,
With each fluffy bite, we soften our grief.

What's the secret to flipping? Is it wrist or a grin?
A sprinkle of laughter, let the chaos begin!
Pancakes piled high can mend the divine,
While syrupy wishes flow freely in line.

With each soft edge, a story unfolds,
Of mornings so bright, where happiness holds.
Let's gather around, share our tales of delight,
For comfort is simple as morning turns bright.

In the warmth of the kitchen, we find our grace,
In fluffy round wonders, we find our place.
So let's lift our forks and ask "What's the deal?"
As the batter of life, we serve up the meal.

Warm Wisdom Wrapped in Flapjacks

In golden brown winks, wisdom is found,
Pancakes whisper secrets as they sizzle around.
What gives life flavor? Is it sweet or it's sour?
With syrupy answers, we embrace our power.

The batter of dreams is mixed just right,
With laughter and courage, we take flight.
Can flipping pancakes teach courage and cheer?
Or is it just breakfast and fun with no fear?

A sprinkle of salt in a world that's too sweet,
Brings balance to plates, so we're never discreet.
In stacks of joy, we ponder and play,
Finding delight in each buttery ray.

So gather your friends, let the pancakes unite,
In fluffy discussions, till the evening light.
For wrapped in each flapjack, a lesson we'll find,
The joy of the moment, in pancakes aligned.

Griddle Wisdom

In the morning light we stand,
With syrup and butter, oh so grand.
What is the meaning, what's the plan?
Flip a pancake, maybe it's a fan.

Drowning in toppings, sweet and warm,
Questions like pancakes take on new form.
Are dreams just fluff, or do they perform?
Watch them rise, like a perfect storm.

With every bite, a riddle unfolds,
What makes us happy? The syrup it holds.
Toppings are secrets, like stories retold,
In the griddle's dance, life's truths unfold.

So grab a fork, hold it high,
For crispy edges that touch the sky.
Who needs answers when flavors fly?
Eat your way through, oh my oh my!

The Breakfast of Contemplation

As dawn's bright light begins to seep,
We ponder pancakes, and they make us weep.
Is happiness simple, or is it deep?
With a side of bacon, maybe we leap.

Stacking our thoughts like layers of dough,
Is it all sweet, or does it go low?
Flipping our minds, letting ideas flow,
With whipped cream clouds, we shine in the glow.

Are we just breakfast, a fading delight?
Or a savory treat, taking flight in the night?
Every pancake whispers, "Hold on tight!"
In syrupy moments, we feel so right.

So scoff the confusion with laughter and cheer,
Each forkful a symbol of wisdom so near.
With laughter and syrup, we banish the fear,
At the table of thoughts, we feast with good cheer.

Pancake Truths

A pancake asks, with its golden face,
"Is there a destination, or just a race?"
Do we stack our dreams, or let them replace?
With a sprinkle of joy, we find our place.

When life gets sticky, and syrup spills wide,
Do we drown our doubts, or take them in stride?
Each layer a lesson, won't let them hide,
Fold in the laughter; let hope be our guide.

With chocolate chips and odd little shapes,
We puzzle our lives like jigsaw scrapes.
Every bite tells a story, no escapes,
In the breakfast hour, wisdom takes shapes.

So grab a plate, and munch with glee,
For pancakes hold secrets, don't you see?
With every warm flip, we're wild and free,
The answers are tasty, let's have a spree!

Stacked Solutions

A tower of pancakes, oh what a sight,
Questions are fluffy, answers take flight.
Do we serve them savory, or sweet delight?
With a dash of laughter, we conquer the night.

The batter of life is messy and bold,
Do we let it rise, or leave it untold?
Syrup like wisdom, it never grows old,
Pour on the sweetness; let stories unfold.

With every new pancake, we shift our view,
Are toppings opinions, or are they for two?
Enjoy every bite, as we savor the hue,
In the stack of solutions, we find what is true.

So here's to the breakfast that brings us together,
Pancakes for thoughts, in all kinds of weather.
With humor and syrup, we're light as a feather,
In the stack of our lives, we'll always endeavor!

Savory Secrets on a Plate

What is joy but fluffy stacks,
With syrup rivers flowing, no lacks.
They hold the secrets, warm and bright,
In bites of gold, our hearts take flight.

Do they ponder, do they care,
If topping dreams are light or rare?
Soft whispers rise with every flip,
In breakfast tales, we freely sip.

A sprinkle here, a dash of that,
Life's funny twists in pancake spat.
With butter smiles and toppings neat,
The answers tease, and then retreat.

So when you're lost and need a clue,
Just stack more pancakes, that's the view.
Each bite a giggle, syrupy cheer,
In every layer, truths appear.

Round and Resilient Queries

What spins our wheels, makes mornings sweet?
Round like sun, a tasty treat.
Each circle maketh worries cease,
In every bite, a bit of peace.

Do they ask about the path ahead?
Or should we just grub instead?
With flourished hearts, we pour the mix,
And watch the silly batter tricks.

A flip of fate, both dizzy and grand,
Each syrup swirl a guiding hand.
As flavors dance on plates of joy,
We find the meaning, oh boy, oh boy!

In golden rounds, the wisdom flows,
Beneath the fluff, who truly knows?
With laughter rising, nothing's bleak,
These pancakes speak, oh how they speak!

Dilemmas on a Hot Plate

Where do we go on a Sunday morn'?
With butter suns to greet the dawn.
Fluffy dilemmas, hot and bright,
Serve them up, we'll take a bite.

Should we add berries, or go plain?
What if the whole stack goes insane?
With each decision, we frown and nod,
Till syrup drips like a bard's prod.

Can we flip our worries high?
While pancakes land, oh me, oh my!
Eggs will crack and bacon sizzle,
But answers form in nudges, drizzle.

So when life cooks up quite a mess,
Stack pancakes high, they'll surely bless.
In everything soft, the meaning's warm,
A tasty hug in every form.

The Stack of Understandings

In a towering stack of griddle delight,
Wisdom stands tall, oh what a sight!
Is this breakfast, or a puzzle grand?
With each forkful, we understand.

What's the secret to courage, dear?
Perhaps it's simply maple cheer.
With whipped cream atop our doubts, we see,
The world looks better, carefree and free.

Life's questions low, on plates so wide,
We laugh and gobble without a guide.
Every bite brings giggles, that's the key,
In layers soft, hilarity's spree.

So stack them high and share the light,
Pancakes hold answers, oh what a bite!
In every morsel, understanding's fun,
With laughter, life's race is often won.

Savory Questions, Sweet Answers

What's the meaning of this mess?
Is it syrup or just stress?
Stacked high on my plate of dreams,
Pancakes whisper funnier themes.

Do we ponder or just munch?
Can we savor every crunch?
With butter mountains to explore,
Our worries fade, who needs more?

Is this breakfast or a quest?
Fluffy clouds put thoughts to rest.
A sprinkle of laughter, light and round,
In syrupy joy, answers are found.

Why so serious, do you say?
Chase the frowns right away.
With every bite, a puzzle solved,
In pancake wisdom, chaos dissolved.

Flapping Thoughts

Thoughts flip like pancakes on the griddle,
Sizzling moments, laughter in the middle.
What's the secret to a smile so wide?
A breakfast stack and a playful side.

Worries whisk away with ease,
Like batter swirling, a playful breeze.
Why do we fret? What's the last call?
Just grab a fork; it's fun for all!

Questions bubble up, all in the pan,
Mixing up answers, who needs a plan?
Is it fortune or just grains of flour?
Each bite a giggle, each hour a power.

Pancakes served with a wink and a smile,
Taste the joy, go on, stay a while.
In fluffy layers, the truth takes flight,
With each syrupy drizzle, our spirits ignite.

The Breakfast of Reflection

Morning sun and syrup beams,
Fluffy clouds filled with dreams.
What's the secret sauce of glee?
Pancakes whisper, come and see!

Fried doubts on a golden plate,
Slice through tension, it's never too late.
Is happiness a pancake stack?
With each bite, we bounce right back!

Jokes are served with every slice,
Laughter drenched in sweetness, oh so nice.
What's the point of all this fun?
In pancake moments, we've already won!

So grab a plate and take a seat,
Join the flavors and the beat.
With pancakes guiding our merry way,
Each question fades like last night's fray.

Filling the Void with Flapjacks

When pondering the big things,
    I pour the batter thick.
With syrup like sweet wisdom,
    Each bite's a little trick.

Questions swirl around my head,
    Like bubbles in the pan.
I flip with hope and humor,
    Just flip it—yes, I can!

The spatula's my guide,
In a world that feels so flat.
One bite of fluff and goodness,
    And suddenly, I'm at.

A plate stacked high with joy,
    It's a remedy for doubt.
    One delicious flapjack,
And life's a happy route.

Pancakes of Purpose

What's my meaning, where's my edge?
I seek in every bite.
The golden brown, my sacred pledge,
I'll flip the day to light.

Batter drips with every question,
And sizzles just like dreams.
The secret's in the texture,
Or so it surely seems.

With butter to top off the quest,
And jam to spread on wide.
I find my answers crispy-fried,
In every syrup slide.

So here's to every riddle,
With syrup on the side.
In fluffy stacks, my answers dwell,
My griddle has my pride.

Maple Musings

In a world of sticky notes,
I find my thoughts take flight.
With every dribble of maple,
I muse into the night.

The pancakes tower high,
Like dreams that touch the sky.
Each layer holds a secret,
Those fluffy clouds pass by.

I ponder every flavor,
The cinnamon and zest.
With each taste, I find my answer,
To what I like the best.

So pour it on with fervor,
And let the skillet gleam.
With every bite, I question,
Am I still in a dream?

The Insightful Griddle

A query springs to batter,
As I stand at the pan.
What's better than a breakfast?
I'm the pancake fan!

With flour dusting wisdom,
I mix my hopes and fears.
In every flip, enlightenment,
And laughter drowns my tears.

The griddle's like a guru,
So hot and full of cheer.
I ask, do pancakes hold truth?
They shout, 'We're always here!'

Syrup flows like answers,
A river sweet and grand.
Each bite a soft reminder,
Life's tasty when you plan.

The Whisk of Wonder

In the morning light, they sizzle and pop,
A breakfast treat, who could ever stop?
With syrup rivers flowing so free,
Pancakes lead us to hilarity.

Toss them high, catch them with flair,
A flip gone wrong? Just laughter in air!
Questions tumble with each pancake stack,
What's the secret? Flip, don't hold back!

Friends gather round, forks raised in delight,
Making memories, everything feels right.
What is wisdom? They softly tease,
A pancake flip can be the best of keys.

So whisk away doubts, let humor abound,
In every fluffy bite, joy can be found.
Maple smiles and giggles unite,
With pancakes in hand, the world feels bright.

Sweet Epiphanies

Golden circles on my plate gleam,
Each bite invites a silly dream.
What's the meaning of success, I ponder,
A stack of pancakes, oh how I wander!

Batter spills like my jumbled thoughts,
Joy served warm in delightful knots.
Do you seek truth? Well, here's a hint:
It's buried deep in that chocolate mint.

Bubbles form and secrets arise,
Pancakes whisper under sunny skies.
Is happiness simply syrupy bliss?
Pour it on thick and you shall not miss!

So flip your worries, let laughter reign,
With each dollop of cream, dissolve the mundane.
In sweet simplicity, fun always dwells,
Pancakes and giggles, oh, what a spell!

Flapjack Queries

Stack them high, a mountain of fluff,
Am I enough? Well, sure, that's tough.
With each golden disc, connections grow,
Pancakes ask truths we're afraid to show.

A sprinkle of nuts, a dollop of jam,
What do you want? Just be who you am!
Each syrupy swipe, a memory made,
In pancake moments, doubts start to fade.

Let's flip for fortune, and see what we find,
What's the recipe for peace of mind?
With laughter bubbling like batter in a bowl,
Pancakes reveal, they nourish the soul.

From breakfast tables, wisdom is served,
With sprinkles of joy, and laughs unreserved.
So ever hungry, take life with a grin,
For flapjacks and fun always win!

Flip and Flow

On the griddle, they glide and spin,
Each flip a question, let's dive right in!
What's the secret to being free?
Just pour some syrup and laugh with glee.

Bubbles pop like thoughts in the air,
Could pancake dreams take us somewhere?
With friends and forks, we share our plight,
Life's puzzles shrink with each tasty bite.

Banana slices or berries so bright,
What brings me joy? Can pancakes ignite?
In each fluffy layer, possibilities bloom,
So feast on the fun, let your worries zoom.

Let's stack our hopes and make them real,
In this pancake paradise, we joyfully feel.
Pour it on thick, let laughter flow,
For every question, there's a pancake show!

Pancakes and Perception

Fluffy stacks on a plate, warm and bright,
They whisper secrets as we chew and bite.
Do they hold truths in their syrupy glaze?
Or just sweet moments that drift in a haze?

A pancake's flip is a turn of fate,
Both crisp and soft, they make us wait.
What's hidden within their golden sheen?
Perhaps the meaning of what might have been.

Each bite a puzzle, a curious quest,
To find the answers or eat what's best.
With laughter and butter, we take a chance,
In the dance of syrup, we make our stance.

So here's to the pancakes, the joy they bring,
In every layer, we find the zing.
Stacked high, they show us life's little quirks,
Let's savor the flavor that truly works!

Battering Doubts

Whisking away all the worries and fears,
A splash of milk to wash down the tears.
Flip those doubts like a pancake right,
Sizzle them crisp in the morning light.

The skillet's hot, and so are we,
Doubts bubble up, oh let them be!
Sprinkle some laughter, a dash of cheer,
With every flip, we turn to our gear.

Calories count, but who really cares?
Pancakes fix everything, lighten our scares.
Turn up the heat, let's have some fun,
As long as we're flipping, we're never done!

So batter your worries, make them smooth,
Join in the dance, find your groove.
With syrupy smiles and a side of glee,
Let's feast on life, just you and me!

The Sweetness of Certainty

In a world of doubts, be like a pancake,
Fluffy and round, never gonna break.
With each syrup drizzle, certainty's near,
A breakfast of peace, let's give a cheer!

Everyone stirs in their own special way,
But the best mixes come fresh every day.
Pour in the laughter, flip out the grey,
For sweetness in life, we'll surely stay.

With chocolate chips or berries galore,
Each bite brings joy we simply can't ignore.
A plate piled high is our secret stash,
Whisk it all together, ready to smash!

So grab your fork and raise a toast,
To certainty wrapped in flavors we boast.
From kitchen to heart, let the love cascade,
In this pancake world, we've got it made!

Golden Grains of Wisdom

Golden grains swirling in a batter delight,
Whip them around till they mingle just right.
What do they teach with their buttery gleam?
Perhaps it's to savor and follow our dream.

With each golden flip, we learn something new,
Like how even burnt can be tasty too!
Wisdom isn't perfect, nor is it plain,
It's sweet in the middle, with edges of grain.

So stack them up high, let's build a tower,
With laughter as syrup, we'll bloom like a flower.
Each layer teaches, no need for a book,
Just look at those pancakes, take a good look!

In morning's soft light, they softly confess,
That golden grains can truly impress.
With each crispy bite, we spread joy like jam,
In the world of pancakes, it's only "yes, ma'am!"

Flour, Sugar, and Answers

Mix in the flour, a dash of thought,
With sugar so sweet, the answers are sought.
Whisk the worries, flip the frown,
Pancakes rise up, never let down.

Pour syrup on truths, smooth and rich,
With each golden flip, find a new pitch.
Fluffy and light, they dance on the plate,
Craving is life, oh, isn't it great?

Butter melts slow, like time on the run,
Each bite a reminder that life can be fun.
Questions dissolve in the warm, sweet haze,
Pancakes, the answer that warrants our praise.

So stack 'em up high, don't fret or despair,
For in every bite, there's love in the air.
With forks held aloft, let laughter commence,
In the world of pancakes, it all makes sense.

Flip Your Thoughts

Flip your thoughts like a pancake's rise,
Up and down, twist and surprise.
Butter and syrup, a playful art,
Each bite of joy, an open heart.

Griddles are hot, but so is the chat,
Toss in some laughter, imagine that!
Questions spin round like batter in need,
Pancakes are wisdom, that's guaranteed.

Crispy edges hug fluffy inside,
Life's little secrets, no need to hide.
Sprinkle some berries, add in a smile,
Enjoying the journey, mile after mile.

So when in a quandary, no need to stare,
Just grab a fork, take a moment to share.
For every dilemma, there's butter to spread,
Flip your thoughts over, feast on your bread.

Comfort in Every Bite

In a world of chaos, grab a plate,
Pancakes offer calm, oh, isn't it great?
They soak up the syrup, like love on a spree,
Each bite a question, answered with glee.

Mixing the batter, a whirl of delight,
Cooking up laughter from morning till night.
When troubles arise, they stack up so high,
A tower of comfort beneath the blue sky.

Flipping nostalgia with butter and cream,
Pancakes are magic, like a sweet dream.
Serving up questions with joy and some flair,
Each fluffy morsel dissolves all the despair.

So eat up the fun, and drown in the sweet,
Life's puzzles unravel with every good treat.
Finding the answers in moments so right,
Comfort is certain, with each pancake bite.

Brunching with Curiosity

Gather 'round people, it's that time again,
Pancakes are calling, let's gather the pen.
Jot down your queries, no need to feel shy,
With syrupy laughter, let questions fly high.

Brunch is the magic where flavors collide,
Flip those pancakes, let curiosity glide.
Whip-up some wonder with blueberries bold,
In the kitchen of wisdom, new stories unfold.

Why is the sky blue, or what makes us cheer?
Stir the batter, dissolve every fear.
Maple or honey, the choices abound,
Answers come easy when pancakes are found.

Next round of flipping, let's do it with flair,
Each stack hides secrets, we'll gladly share.
So laugh while you nibble, be curious too,
With pancakes and friends, there's no tale untrue.

www.ingramcontent.com/pod-product-compliance
Lightning Source LLC
Chambersburg PA
CBHW072214070526
44585CB00015B/1329